SMUTS MEM

GU00983127

FIFTY
OF
COMMONWEALTH
ECONOMIC
DEVELOPMENT

BY

AUSTIN ROBINSON

C.M.G., F.B.A.

Emeritus Professor of Economics
in the University of Cambridge

CAMBRIDGE

AT THE UNIVERSITY PRESS

1972

Published by the Syndics of the Cambridge University Press
Bentley House, 200 Euston Road, London NW1 2DB
American Branch: 32 East 57th Street, New York, N.Y. 10022

© Cambridge University Press 1972

ISBN: 0 521 08577 2

Printed in Great Britain
at the University Printing House, Cambridge
(Brooke Crutchley, University Printer)

I

I HAVE chosen to speak tonight on the subject of 'Fifty Years of Commonwealth Economic Development' for two reasons, one personal, one more substantial. My personal reason, perhaps properly irrelevant on such an occasion as this, is that fifty years almost exactly spans my own working life as an economist, so that I can use my own memory to supplement and interpret the literature. The more substantial, and to my mind much more relevant, reason is that the early years of the 1920s represent, I think, a watershed, ill-defined and at first scarcely perceptible, between the period of the development of the Old Commonwealth – call it if you will the White Commonwealth – and the period in which our chief concentration has been on the development of the New Commonwealth – the Commonwealth of Asia, Africa and the Caribbean.

In the Commonwealth development of the nineteenth century and the first fourteen years of this century, Britain played a dominant part as source of capital, as supplier of necessary capital goods, as source of trained manpower and of technical knowledge for new industrial enterprises. But it would never have occurred to a contemporary Englishman looking at this (it certainly never occurred to me researching into it in 1922) to regard it as charity, as 'aid' in the language of today. It was hard-headed business enterprise, handsomley rewarded where successful, unrewarded – for much of it was equity investment – where the enterprise was ill-conceived or ill-managed. It is a paradox that much that today passes as 'aid' with its connotation of altruism, is in performance, if not in concept, less altruistic, more exigent of unconditional payment of interest and capital, than the hard-headed and self-seeking enterprise of the nineteenth century.

The Commonwealth was not the only beneficiary of British nineteenth-century foreign investment and foreign enterprise. Much went to Europe. The United States continued to attract British capital throughout the railway building age and much later. So did Latin America. Of the total British foreign investment outside Europe before 1870, a little over half (51%) was in the United States and Latin America. Of the 49% inside what was later to become the Commonwealth, Canada, Australasia and South Africa had taken 20%; India had absorbed 29%. Fifteen years later, in 1885, the share of the USA and Latin America was down to 40%, that of India had fallen to 24%. Canada, Australasia and the Cape had gone up from 20% to 34%. Of the increment from 1870 to 1885, these countries had taken almost a half.

If we move on to 1911, estimates for that year (not

strictly comparable, but sufficiently so for the very broad comparison that I am attempting), would suggest that of the total aid that we had provided down to that date, about 47% had gone to the United States and Latin America, about 41% to the White Commonwealth. India's share had fallen to about 13% from the 29% it represented in 1870. She had drawn quite heavily on us for a period in 1860–90, while the railways were building and during the period of active development that followed; but thereafter our contribution to her slow development was relatively slight down to 1914, and far later. African development was mostly in the Cape, Natal and the Transvaal and associated with minerals and railways, though Rhodes' enthusiasm for railway building and early mineral developments began to move the area that was benefiting up into Central Africa by the 1990s.

But the picture of pre-1921 development that I think I am right to draw is one of a quite remarkable British contribution to world development, with the Americas and the White Commonwealth as the principal beneficiaries. I call it a remarkable contribution advisedly. Today we struggle to make a somewhat similar contribution of aid to developing nations equivalent to 1% of gross national product. Over the whole fifty-year period 1865–1914, our average ratio of foreign investment to gross national product was no less than 4·3%; for the years 1905–14 it was 6·8%. I shall have something to say later about the circumstances in which this was achieved and the consequences for ourselves as well as for others.

The benefits of our nineteenth-century aid were widely spread, but none-the-less remarkably effective in promoting the growth of the economies of the recipient countries. The reason is not far to seek. The British national income of the time was far larger in proportion to those of the recipient countries than is our income today in relation to those we are trying to help. A very rough estimate suggests that the British national income was about four times the sum of the national incomes of the Commonwealth countries we were principally aiding in 1880. Today it is slightly less on the one hand than the total of the Old Commonwealth and slightly more (about 5% more) than the total of the New, predominantly Asian and African, Commonwealth – equal that is to say to a little less than half that of the whole of the rest of the Commonwealth.

One can see this also in terms of population. The total population of the principal Commonwealth beneficiaries of our late nineteenth-century aid (excluding India which as I have said was a relatively small beneficiary) amounted in 1880 to about 35% of the United Kingdom population; in 1911 to about 41%. To such countries we could provide aid in amounts that were large enough to make significant contributions to their economies. The £1,100 millions that we had invested in Australasia, Canada and South Africa down to 1911 represented about £60 per head of their population. The annual inflow in the 1880s and 1890s represented about half the value of their total fixed investment during those years.

II

I have said that the early 1920s represented a watershed, perhaps ill-defined and at the time hardly perceptible, between nineteenth-century Commonwealth development and what we have now come to regard as the mid-twentieth-century pattern; the first a hard-headed rather strictly economic development of the Old Commonwealth; the second a more emotional and supposedly more altruistic development of the New Commonwealth.

The outpouring of funds to develop the Old Commonwealth came to an abrupt end in the 1920s because we no longer had the funds to outpour. The change was as traumatic, and possibly more permanent, than the change in dollar affluence in the past year. The 1914–18 War had permanently changed the whole basis of the British balance of payments. Down to 1913 a persistently favourable balance of payments was the happy result of two things: the large inflow of profits, interest and dividends from overseas, and the continued sale of our textile and coal exports. Both disappeared with the war. The foreign income, as the result of sales of foreign securities and of rising prices, was reduced considerably in purchasing power. The sales of cotton textiles were never again to exceed 66% of the 1913 volume. From 1921 onwards we were persistently struggling to achieve a minimum balance without any surplus for investment.

The repercussions in the Old Commonwealth were not serious. We had nursed them through what Rostow has identified as their periods of 'take-off'. Their growth could now begin to be 'self-sustained'. Australia, New Zealand and South Africa, though they continued to draw on us, drew less heavily. Canada had become virtually self-supporting or dependent on American funds.

The contemporary change of our attitudes to Commonwealth development was not only enforced by our change of circumstances. It was reinforced by a change in our philosophy and thinking about the problems facing those countries of what was to become the New Commonwealth that remained heavily dependent upon us.

The beginnings of the new philosophy and ideology of Commonwealth development are largely unidentified and unrecorded. I am unaware of having thought deeply about them or of having analysed them at the time, though I can now realise in retrospect my own shifts of thinking. They began, I think, as the counterpart of the similar thinking on the political front, particularly in the African setting, with Lugard's early emphasis on the dual mandate and the equality, later the paramountcy, of native

African interests – thinking that developed through the Churchill White Paper of 1927, the Hilton Young Commission of 1929, the Passfield White Paper of 1930. It was reinforced by the sense of responsibility for native African interests imposed by the Permanent Mandates Commission of the League of Nations. Certainly by the mid-1930s, when I first began to work with Lord Hailey on his *African Survey*, we assumed the paramountcy of African native welfare as one of the axioms of all our work. And through that work, as well as at first hand, we came to realise the similar streams of thought, sometimes by hindsight over-paternalistic but none-the-less sincere, in the minds of the best of the French and Belgian administrators.

That represented, I believe, one early tributary to the new thinking. Another tributary, I think, was the evolution in economic thinking that we associate with the name of Maynard Keynes. The Keynesian revolution proper was concerned with employment theory, but its ramifications were enormously wider; for what we learned, or taught ourselves, as the result of that revolution was that many things which hitherto were regarded as fate, as part of the given data of economics, were in fact changeable, were things that we could control and guide. We had hitherto regarded the wealth or poverty of nations and their rates of growth as things which were in the main given, alterable perhaps in small degree and over long periods by wise or foolish economic

9

policies; but in the main to be regarded as fate, as the given data. We began to see them as things that were alterable. But once one came to regard things as alterable, one came to regard them as things for which one had a responsibility. If they were evil things, like poverty, one had a responsibility to do what was in one's power to mitigate them. I think this is a change in the lifetimes of many of us here that has never been adequately recorded or even appreciated.

A third tributary to thinking about the problems of developing the New Commonwealth derived, I would suggest, from the growth of thought and action in the field of welfare services and redistributional taxation that started, perhaps, with Lloyd George's 1911 Budget, developed progressively through the inter-war years, and found its climax in the post-1946 extensions of welfare services. It was very natural to extend this thinking – and socialist literature very quickly did – to redistribution between rich countries and poor countries. One finds it in the contemporary writing of Brailsford and Rita Hinden, for example, and it obviously affected Sidney Webb's (Lord Passfield's) thinking.

Of these three streams, I find it as impossible, as with the White Nile and the Blue Nile, to identify the main river. By the outbreak of war, they were all making their contributions to the whole flow of thinking. But at the time that I worked with Lord Hailey in 1935–8 our thinking was still more static, more concerned with minor but important reforms, more tolerant of quasi-permanent differences between nations than it would have been if we had written the same study ten years later, still more so if we had written it twenty years later.

Whence then came the difference? I think that, as so often, it came from two sources. The first was a revitalising of all the thinking of the Colonial Office. From where that came I cannot pretend to know. But serving on a variety of Colonial Office Committees in the years during and just after the 1939–45 War, I came to associate it with the dynamism of Andrew Cohen. Just as one came in wartime to regard all problems as soluble, given the will to solve them, so we were being made to look at the problems of colonial development as potentially soluble problems, and our tasks as the problems of defining the ways in which they could be solved.

The second difference was the gradual emergence during these years of an economic theory of growth – perhaps in the presence of a number of economists I should more accurately say a profusion of theories of growth. Of these, I shall have more to say later.

For the moment may I continue to look at the intellectual changes – the changes of attitude? I would want to argue that by 1939 we had the impulse, the concern to do more about the development of the New Commonwealth. By 1946 we had in addition the determination to do it and a belief that we knew how to do it.

At that stage the development of the theory of growth was in retrospect naive, brash, over-confident. The emphasis was on the relation of capital investment to growth. Most of us who were seeking to apply the ideas of our theoretical colleagues to advising particular countries were thinking crudely in terms of the overall capital/output ratios required for growth, and blithely assumed that a sufficient supply of capital was not merely the *sine qua non* which it almost certainly is, but also in a full and complete sense a *causa causans*, which it almost certainly is not.

It did not take very long for the failures of certain countries to develop as expected and the researches of economists into explanations of growth to show us that this initial emphasis on capital flows was not the whole truth. For a time some of us tried to rescue this first line of approach by being more specific about capital requirements for particular activities. But the testing of theories of growth by application to countries like the United States or the United Kingdom with long runs of data quickly showed that capital investment alone would explain less than a quarter of all growth (in the United States less than a fifth).

Thus we found ourselves trying to explain the other three-quarters of growth. I shall not try – this is no occasion for it – to appraise the attempts that have been made to do this or the validity of the assumptions that underlie them. Sufficient to say that these attempts have sought to allocate shares in the explanation of progress not only to capital, but also to such things as economies of scale of production, education, technical progress, research and development, changes in the effective working week, and so on.

What is more important is that the ever-zealous officials of the United Nations, of UNESCO, of OECD have hastened to sell prematurely to developing countries all the latest and most fashionable medicines of this ever-enlarging pharmacopoeia. For a period salvation through education was the favourite theory; for another period the transmission of technology. Those of us who have been more concerned to understand and interpret have found ourselves increasingly sceptical, or perhaps more properly agnostic. I myself – as one of the officers of the International Economic Association – have been involved for fifteen years past in this pursuit of the will-o'-the-wisp of the unexplained factor. I can only say that at the end of that time I feel less confident that I know how to explain growth than when I started.

It is perhaps a commentary on this that at the end of a conference this summer on the contribution of research and development to growth we found ourselves unable to attribute any large responsibility to this and speculating as to whether incentives, the quality of entrepreneuring, and the like are not of greater importance than had been supposed – we found ourselves, that is to say, coming back nearer to the thinking of the economic historians. But what I think needs to be said is this. We know fairly clearly the factors that are significant. We do not yet know their interconnections – how far for instance, new advances in technology must inevitably be embodied in capital, in expenditure on education and training, in research into local adaptation, to make them fully effective. Nor do we know how to prescribe for a particular country at a particular moment of time, the exact mixture of policies which will be most effective. Wisdom and judgement have still a very important role in the making of economic policy.

III

Over the past fifty years, I have attempted to argue, we have found a new determination to help the development of the New Commonwealth and a new body of knowledge to help us to achieve it. How far has this been paralleled by a corresponding growth of achievement?

Let me go back then to the 1920s and 1930s and look at what we were then doing and at what was happening. The ideas of redistribution and of assistance to developing countries were germinating. But they were very far from affecting practical policies. The working philosophy of those years was that countries should, save in circumstances of extreme difficulty, pay their way. As late as 1937 the Economic Survey of the Colonial Empire was taking pride in the fact, for example, that 'no grant in aid had been given to Uganda since 1915' and that its free grants from the Colonial Development Fund for the whole period from 1930 to 1937, mostly for services on the air route to the Cape, had scarcely exceeded £20,000. It was not to be thought that the Treasury, engaged in curing unemployment over those years by cutting expenditures, would welcome new claimants on its funds. The position is well illustrated by a table in the first edition of the Hailey Survey which estimates the total funds available in African territories for all government expenditures on economic development and social services together; they range from about 1·8 shillings a head annually for Nigeria and Nyasaland to 7·4 shillings a head for the comparatively affluent Gold Coast, with Kenya, Uganda and Northern Rhodesia in the range of 3·4 to 4·8 shillings. On such expenditures the development policies were inevitably simple and constricted. It was only in the 1950s that we began to learn to think in millions of pounds.

This does not mean that nothing was being done for development. It means only that what was done was very largely done from the exiguous funds of the dependencies themselves. Over these years the most important contribution to development was the building up of the agricultural services. Agriculture represented in many African countries nine-tenths of all activity and more than half of all income. Thus

15

it was natural to give it priority. My impressions of the agricultural research stations of the 1930s were of the very high quality of the almost wholly expatriate research staff, of the gains from close contacts of these expatriates with the research institutes of the mother country, and of their dedicated interest in their work and in solving the difficult problems of animal diseases, of the introduction of new cash crops and of the improvement of methods of cultivation. While agricultural research expenditures have multiplied many times in recent years, I cannot but feel that much of it is less well directed and less effective than that of the 1930s. We now take for granted the new cash crops, the improvements of animal husbandry that flowed from that work.

Education during the 1920s and 1930s was slow to advance. In Africa it was almost wholly concentrated, so far as Africans were concerned, in the hands of the missionaries. Anyone who travelled, as I did in the early 1930s, the missionary schools of Central Africa, was torn between admiration of how much they were doing with such inadequate funds and disappointment that little more could be attempted, save for a few fortunates who were sent abroad, than the barest literacy. Yet it was in those mission schools that most of the African leaders of today received a background of education that has left an imprint on them through life. In Asia education had reached much higher levels half a century earlier. But here too lack of facilities and trained staff meant all too often that the education was too narrowly academic and literary, with relatively little science teaching outside the medical schools, and ill adapted to the emerging needs of such a country as India, so that a first task since independence has been to change the scope and emphasis of the education system.

In one respect the pre-1939 development was more far reaching and permanent in its effects. The first prerequisite of modern development in all these countries of the New Commonwealth was an infra-structure which would permit the movement of imports and exports and provide the necessary public utility services of water, electricity, sewage in the growing cities. By 1913 there already existed almost the whole of the present railway systems of India and Pakistan – these date principally from the 1860s to 1880s – and those of the African commonwealth countries, which date chiefly from the 1900s. Of the total of British overseas investment down to 1913 about 24% went directly to railways and a large fraction of the 44% borrowed by governments went indirectly to railway construction. As compared with the railway systems, the road systems remained extraordinarily primitive. By the 1930s few of the roads of Central Africa were all-weather roads or could move goods throughout the year. The modernisation of the road systems in Africa, as in Asia, has remained a task for the 1950s and 1960s. Electricity supplies in the major towns were beginning to be taken for granted by the 1930s. They were, it is true, small scale, high cost and sub-

17

ject – then as now – to frequent overloading and failure. Over these years, again, the port facilities of most of these countries had been developed to the point where they could handle the rapidly growing exports and imports. One must not exaggerate the perfection of the infra-structure which had been created over these years. Nor on the other hand must one forget that by the beginning of the 1950s many of the prerequisites for more rapid and more industrial development were already in existence.

Through the 1920s and 1930s the industrialisation of the New Commonwealth advanced very slowly. In Africa small-scale craftsmanship was being taught in the mission schools; larger scale industry was almost confined to the railway workshops and the work-shops attached to the mining companies. In India, it is true, industrial production was much older than British rule. Textiles, small engineering workshops, craftsmanship in wood and stone had flourished and later declined through competition with British and other imports. But in the climate of *laisser faire* principles new industries were difficult to get started. There had been exceptions, particularly in textiles, when profits were high, as in the cotton mills of Bombay and Ahmedabad and the jute mills of Cal-cutta. But larger scale metal and engineering indus-tries were slow to develop, outside the railway work-shops. The watershed was marked by reports of the Indian Fiscal Commission of 1921–2 and the appoint-ment of a Tariff Board in 1923. The Industrial Commission which had produced an interesting and valuable report five years earlier in 1918 had been precluded by its terms of reference from suggesting forms of encouragement that were 'incompatible with the existing fiscal policy of the Government of India' – a provision which did not prevent Pandit Malaviya from advocating policies in a separate note which could scarcely have been implemented without a change of these policies. From 1924 onwards assistance in tariff and other forms to new industries or to existing industries in need of support was at least possible. But it was administered by a Tariff Board steeped in the earlier traditions, and applications were more often rejected than accepted. Steel, paper and various chemical industries were among the relatively few important beneficiaries.

IV

How far can we measure the rate of progress during the first twenty of the fifty years that I am attempting to survey – from 1920, or better 1913, that is, to 1940? How does this growth compare with what had gone before and what was to come after? For India alone of the countries of the New Commonwealth can one attempt, thanks to Mukerjee and the predecessors on whom he draws, a long period estimate covering the whole economy. If one takes the whole period of ninety years, 1860–1950 – that is to say down to the beginning of Indian post-independence planned development, helped by the Colombo Plan and American aid – the average rate of total national income growth was a little under 1.2% a year. The growth of income per head averaged less than 0.5% a year over ninety years as a whole, and the growth of population over the ninety years averaged about 0.7% a year. But the advances of medicine had progressively increased the rate of growth of population from 0.4% in the first 25 years to 0.8% in the final 35 years, and growth of income per head had progressively declined from about 1.0% in the first 25 years to little more than 0.1% in the period 1915 to 1950 – a state perilously near to stagnation, which contributed not a little to political clamour on the one hand and to despair and fatalism on the other.

In Africa we have serious estimates only for the Union. Frankel's calculations indicate that over the period from 1911/12 to 1938/9 the economy as a whole grew by about 3.9% a year and income per head by about 1.7% a year. For the rest of Africa we have not, and probably never can have, similar estimates. The necessary data were never collected and do not exist today. Thus one can do no more than make such inferences and guesses as are possible from the evidence that is available from statistics of values and tonnages of exports, tonnages carried by railways, tonnages of shipping movements, population data and the like. I have tried for the purposes of this lecture to attempt to make estimates. I think that certain conclusions are reasonably firm. In a number of African Commonwealth countries the rate of growth from 1913 to 1937 was high, and I would believe higher than the growth of recent years. In particular, Ghana (the Gold Coast as it then was) grew more rapidly from 1913 to 1937 than from 1950 to 1968 both in total income and especially in income per head. Nigeria was probably growing about 2·0% to 2·5% per annum in 1913–37 and has greatly accelerated. Kenya and Uganda were probably growing a little less rapidly in 1913–37 than today, but with less rapid population growth, their annual growth of income per head was then probably greater (I estimate it at about 2·6%) than it has been in 1950–68.

I am very aware of the limitations of my attempts to estimate. But I would stress one point which I believe to be certain – that it is very wrong to generalise in regard to Africa that 1945 represents a point of change from stagnation to progress. It is true that the depression of 1932–3 hit Africa very severely. But in all countries that I have studied, income per head almost certainly rose significantly between 1929 and 1937.

May I come next to what has been happening since 1950? Despite the scepticism or agnosticism which I have expressed about the adequacy of our present knowledge of the causes and recipes for development, world growth has been more rapid and more consistent, and within it the countries of the New Commonwealth, except in years of famine, disaster and war, have advanced faster. The greatest contrast is in India and Pakistan. The average rate of total growth from 1950 to 1968 has been about three times that of 1913–37. The growth of income per head, despite faster population growth, has been more than eight times greater.

In Africa the increases have been less spectacular but none-the-less very marked. In South Africa, total growth has risen from 3·8% to 4·9%; that of income per head from 1·7% to 2·5%. Such a difference may sound small. But it represents the difference between doubling income per head in 28 and in 42 years. Elsewhere in Africa it is more difficult to generalise. In Nigeria the increase in growth has been marked – close to a doubling of the growth of income and more than a doubling of the growth of income per head. Ghana, in terms of income per head, has recently been stagnating. Kenya and Uganda have continued to advance but I would believe a little less rapidly than in 1913–37.

V

How far have these higher rates of growth of the countries of the New Commonwealth meant that the gap between rich and poor has been narrowed? The answer depends on the exact question that is asked. In almost all the countries of the New Commonwealth the total national growth has been faster than that of the United Kingdom. But because our population growth has been lower, our income per head has been growing faster than that of many of them.

But I find this type of calculation misleading and unrewarding. With Professor Chenery I would regard the significant question as a different one: How long will it be at current and expected rates of growth before these countries reach a tolerable standard of life – a level which Chenery takes to be an income of $800 a year at 1967 prices – a level half way between that of Greece and Italy, close to that of Spain, very close to the real income of this country in 1929 – an income which, let me hasten to say, is marginally tolerable rather than desirable? In 1940, at then existing rates of growth, India was almost infinitely removed from that state of semi-bliss. With income per head rising 35% per century, it would have taken her eight centuries to reach it. Today, with the much faster growth rate achieved in recent years, she remains some $1\frac{3}{4}$ centuries remote. If the target increase of income per head of the present plan can be fulfilled, she would still be eighty years distant. Countries in Africa, growing much faster, are much nearer to the $800 level. Nigeria, if she could continue her present growth, would reach it in about 65 years. What is important is that, with the more rapid growth since 1950, this interval of time has been very greatly diminished.

VI

How much of this increase of growth has been due to aid? This is a question that it is not easy to answer. For aid not only provides part of the capital required for growth, but also helps countries to solve the balance of payments problems that represent a constraint on growth. But one can illustrate from the case of India the contribution made to the financing of capital formation. Slightly over one fourth of Indian investment in recent years has been financed by foreign aid. If India could not have financed this otherwise, the rate of total growth might have been nearer to $2 \cdot 5\%$ than $3 \cdot 5\%$ and growth of income per head might have been $0 \cdot 3\%$ rather than $1 \cdot 3\%$ – about the rate of growth of 1885–1915. In terms of the changes of income per head the contribution of aid has quite certainly been very significant.

But we have to ask ourselves whether even the increase achieved will continue to satisfy their aspirations and our consciences. All these countries are looking jealously at Japan, with its total growth of $9 \cdot 6\%$ and its growth of income per head of $8 \cdot 4\%$ from 1952 to 1968, its income per head well above the $800 level, and now approaching that of Italy and Austria and at recent rates of growth only about five years short of overtaking Britain. They are asking themselves why they too cannot progress at similar pace. Part of the answer is, of course, the very low rate of population growth in Japan and all its concomitants – that instead of having to devote something like half of investment to meet the needs of growing population, less than a quarter is so required and a given level of investment will increase productivity by something like 50% more. But this does not explain the whole, or anything like it, of the remarkable performance of Japan.

Of this aid, how much have we contributed? For the Old Commonwealth in the nineteenth century, we were the main source of funds for development. Of the bilateral aid to India and Pakistan in 1965–8 (the latest years analysed in detail) we contributed about 7%; Canada contributed another 7%; 71% came from the United States. Of the bilateral aid to the rest of the Commonwealth we contributed in those years 47%; Canada and Australia contributed 6%; the United States 31%. In each case multilateral aid through the World Bank, IDA, and similar organisations added about 17% to the total of bilateral aid.

Today the future of United States contributions to the development of the New Commonwealth is seriously in doubt. Is there, then, grave danger that the rate of development of the New Commonwealth may slow down rather than increase, just at the moment that the very authoritative Commission under Lester Pearson's chairmanship has been emphasising the need to increase aid, and in particular the official aid, which represents about three-fifths of the whole? May I try to put this problem into perspective? Of all foreign aid to all countries including private investment the United States has provided about 45%; of official aid about 50%, though in proportion to national income American aid has not been large – not as large as our own. The American bilateral aid, which is being cut, represents about half of all American official aid, and rather more than one third of all American aid, including private investment. The 30% cuts proposed by Congress would reduce the total of all American aid by about 10% and reduce the world total of all aid by about 5%. If one narrows one's view to the Commonwealth, the United States in the years 1965–8 – the latest for which we have detailed analysis – provided 60% of the official aid. We provided 16% and Canada and Australia brought this up to 22%. If American cuts are distributed as we expect, the Commonwealth as a whole may lose nearly 20% of the bilateral aid it has been receiving – equivalent to rather more than 10% of all aid.

Two questions must be asked: must this mean a fall in the rates of growth of the Commonwealth Countries? Is there more that we can and should be doing? To the first question I would answer that there are certain rays of hope. Over the past two decades many of the Commonwealth countries have used their aid to build up the infra-structure and basic industries they need and to modify their economic structures so that they are less dependent on imports.

They have also learned to finance more of growth from their internal sources. The effects of the cuts may be less grave than they would have been five years ago. But we had been hoping that these same improvements would lead to faster growth.

VII

Can we ourselves do more? If we attempted to take on our shoulders the whole task of replacing these American cuts so far as they fall on the Commonwealth, it would mean raising our present official aid from its recent 0.4% of gross national product to more than 0.8%. The target for official aid that the Pearson Commission proposed is 0.7%. It would be a very severe task for us to assume individually, but not an impossible task, given the determination to assume it. It is a task, which, in collaboration with other developed nations, is well within our capacity. I think we should be asking ourselves today whether it is not our duty to give a lead to other developed countries in assuming it.

But why should it be so difficult to do more to help the New Commonwealth? If in the nineteenth century we were able to help the Old Commonwealth to 'take-off into self-sustained growth', why, now that we are richer at mid-twentieth century, cannot we do the same for the New Commonwealth? There are, I would suggest, three reasons why it is much

27

more difficult. All of them are implicit in what I have already said.

First, the starting points of the New Commonwealth are very different from those of the Old Commonwealth. Already in 1870, the average incomes per head of Canada, Australia and New Zealand were higher than our own. They were advanced as we were in technology. All that they needed to move on from their agricultural beginnings to their full development as modern industrial nations was the capital to provide a modern infra-structure of transportation, energy supplies and capital equipment. And because they were as highly developed as ourselves and shared our educational and technical backgrounds, our own technologies could be transplanted without problems. The average of the incomes per head of the New Commonwealth is wholly different – about one fifteenth of our own. Their needs are different. Their appropriate technologies if they are to solve their problems of employment are different. The climates and environments are different.

Second, in the late nineteenth century we succeeded in lifting to the point of take-off some 8 million people in the Old Commonwealth, and contributed to the take-off of another 40 million in the United States – about one quarter as many in the Old Commonwealth as in this country. Today we are trying, with the help of the United States and Europe, to give a new dynamic impulse to a New Commonwealth which numbers some 700 million inhabitants.

In the nineteenth century, as I said earlier, the total of the national incomes of the Old Commonwealth was about 25% of our own. Today our own national income is little more than one third of the total of the national incomes of the whole Commonwealth. It is only 6% more than the total of the New Commonwealth that we are anxious to help. Aid which would increase the level of their investment by 25% would require (if we could attempt to shoulder the burden alone) an annual outpouring equal to some 4·2% of our national income – as high a ratio that is to say as the average of the years 1875–1914.

Third, and to my mind by far the greatest obstacle, is the change in the whole domestic setting of the problem. I spoke earlier of the change that the Keynesian economics of our generation has brought to our whole attitude to Commonwealth development. But we have to remember that it has brought the same change to our thinking about our own national development. The nineteenth-century torrent of foreign investment was associated with a decline in the rate of growth of the British economy itself which economic historians are still struggling to explain. Over the decade 1904–14, when British foreign investment was at its peak, the British gross national product grew by an average of about 1·5% a year, and consumption per head by no more than 0·8% a year. Contrast these figures with the history of the 20 years 1950–70: an average growth of gross national product by about 2·7%, of consumption per head by just under 2% – a rate of growth almost universally regarded as very inadequate. One can no longer do good by stealth. Such a domestic stagnation as permitted the investment of 1900–14 would today, when we are convinced that these things can be controlled and averted, bring governments crashing. If we are to do good today, we must do it openly, above board, as a deliberate act of public policy.

May I come back then in conclusion to what seem to me the big issues of today? We are able in this generation to do far more than could our predecessors, partly because we have greater resources, partly because we have a greater understanding, even if it falls short of completeness, of the processes that lead to development. But we, not only in Britain but also in America and other countries, live in an age in which we cannot do good by stealth. Public money and official aid is necessary. It cannot be committed without a public will to do so. Until lately the United States has been doubly important: not only as the provider of half of the total aid, but also, and I would feel even more importantly, as giving an effective moral leadership to the world in this task. Today we fear that the United States, faced by a grave economic crisis which earns our sympathy, will not only be unable to respond to the promptings of the Pearson report but will find itself, temporarily at least, actually cutting its already relatively low level of official aid. More serious, with its eyes inevitably on its own internal situation, the United States Congress seems to me – I hope I am wrong – to be abdicating its world leadership in helping the progress of all developing countries, and not least the poor and populous countries of our own Commonwealth.

In these circumstances I hope that we in Britain may not hesitate to accept the responsibility of giving a leadership to the developed world and of continuing to plead the duty to narrow the gap between rich and poor nations and the duty to help the poorer countries of the Commonwealth to reach within a measurable period of time a standard of life what may be tolerable. I would like to feel that we here in Cambridge, who have educated so many of the leaders of the developing New Commonwealth, may in the spirit and tradition of Smuts ourselves give this lead.

THIS SMUTS MEMORIAL LECTURE WAS
DELIVERED IN THE UNIVERSITY OF CAMBRIDGE
ON 23 NOVEMBER 1971